A Kiss for Grand-darling

a love story

Edwina Gary

Copyright © 2008 Edwina Gary
All rights reserved.

ISBN: 1-4196-5666-X
ISBN-13: 9781419656668

Visit www.booksurge.com to order additional copies.

Dedication

This book is dedicated to my daughter, Angela, to my precious grandchildren, "snugglebug" and "cuddlebug," to my mother, Minnie Gardner Smith, and to my Grand-darling, Ada Gardner.

Prologue

Scientists say that it is the position of the earth and its rotation around the sun that causes the seasons, the life and death cycle of plants. They say that in certain places the sunlight falls in a certain spot, creating a specific picture unlike any other, anywhere on earth.

That's why I will always treasure my childhood and my youth spent in Thomasville, Georgia. There, the sunlight fell in a very special way: on the trees in Grand-darling's back yard; on my mother's gardenias, azaleas, and roses in our front yard; through the trees and moss onto the sparkling white sand of the riverbank; on me, and in my heart. For me, Thomasville will always be home. I can see it, always, in my mind's eye. I can feel its warmth, the sunshine, the light. God's light first touched me in Thomasville.

I first knew music in Thomasville. Grand-darling's upright piano produced a special sound when I touched it the very first time. So gleeful and happy was I that I tried to cover all the keys with my tiny hands. I wanted to hear more. I banged louder and louder with both hands, wanting everyone else to hear more. I didn't know it then, but our desire for other people to hear our own music, the music that we can make, is almost primal.

I first knew silence in Thomasville. Silence gave me the sounds of running water as the river flowed, of birds singing, leaves rustling, dogs barking, trains whistling, rain falling on a tin roof. In silence, I came to know the sound of my own heartbeat when I covered my ears tightly while fearing the dark. Silence gave me the sound of my first baby's heartbeat…

xoxoxoxo

She gave the immediate appearance of a strong woman, and she was. Her five-foot-ten-inch frame dwarfed many of the women of her time. It was also clear that she was a no-nonsense woman; a woman, like so many of us, who had withstood.

She lived in a very close neighborhood, Negro and white. It had been that way since my grandfather purchased the house around 1919. After completing her chores, she'd sit

A Kiss for Grand-darling

on her front porch in her rocking chair, hum her favorite hymns, and talk to neighbors passing by. Sometimes, she'd just rock, in silence.

She was standing behind her front screen door when she fell. Her neighbor, crossing to her yard, looked back just in time to see her fall.

Miss Nancy ran home, and after calling for help, she called the school to have the principal find Minnie Lee to say, "Miss Ada has been taken to the hospital." My grand-darling died when she was seventy-nine years old. For too many years after her death, my mother feared that she would not live past seventy-nine years.

My grand-darling died in October 1966. In July 1967, nine months later, Angela was born. A heart stopped beating, and another heartbeat began. And now, another…

The Kiss

The woman smiled in her sleep. She was dreaming. She smiled again. In her in-between dream state, she was trying to be sure she'd remember every detail of this special dream. She wanted nothing to slip away. This was one of those rare moments in one's lifetime, when everything seems suspended in time and joy falls softly on every part of one, inside and out, like a sudden summer rain. In her bed, in the silence, replaying every little element of this dream in her head, her heart, and her soul was so essential—this was such a wonderful moment!

The woman smiled again. Was she still dreaming, or basking in the memory of the dream? It mattered, and it didn't; this moment was for now, but this dream carried stardust swirls for lifetimes past, present, and future.

The room had a soft ambiance, somewhat like the billows of clouds. The air was calm. The peace of the early morning bedroom was quickly filled with a greater sense of calm, stillness. Suddenly, like a falling star far up in the sky, a baby descended. Out of nowhere it just appeared and hovered, eye to eye, its soft breath bringing love and life to the woman in bed. For a few seconds, they exchanged breaths, rhythmically. Then, looking into the woman's eyes, the baby kissed her. It was one of those soft, hollow kisses; the kind mothers never forget—a warm, open-mouthed kiss from lips and gums. Almost as soon as their lips touched, the baby's mouth pulled back into a wide, glowing smile. For a moment, their eyes met and their hearts met. The woman touched her lips; soft, warm, and now, sacred. The baby had just delivered a kiss for grandma.

I awoke with a smile. I would never be the same again. I remembered. Because of a dream, I was now and forever "Grandma"!

I'm relatively normal, whatever that is. I had a relatively good upbringing in a relatively stable home, with two loving and well-meaning parents. I finished college and went on to marry and raise kids of my own.

In this early morning, sleepy state, I lingered in bed, needing to understand the meaning of my dream. Did it have any real meaning at all? I wondered. Was the baby in the dream a boy or a girl? I really couldn't tell from the dream. Would the baby visit me again in a dream? I certainly hoped it would, because deep down inside I could think of nothing more that would give me such joy!

As far as I could remember, I'd had only one other dream that made such a deep and lasting impression on me. I must have been about twelve or thirteen years old when I had the dream. In that dream, I saw a tall man standing on a pier, his hands in his pockets. He looked deep into my eyes and gave me a one-sided smile. It was what I later called a Victor Mature smile. Victor Mature was a movie star in the fifties who, to my mind, had the most attractive one-sided smile, ever! I was now married to the man in my dream. His top lip kind of curled up and pulled to one side when he smiled,

Anyway, until now, I had not had another dream that felt so prophetic. I felt it inside and out. It made such an impression. It was more like an imprint. I could feel the baby in my blood, as if a part of it was now racing through my veins. I got chills at the thought. Not even the experience of having my own children created such a soul-to-soul connection. I also wondered if, when the baby was born, it would know me and remember the kiss somewhere deep in its soul. Was I now in the baby's "blood," so to speak?

The thought of blood came to mind, in a family sense. I had always heard that "blood is thicker than water." Was "the kiss" where it all started? Did other grandmas get the kiss? I surmised that the kiss was our first hello, properly ordained and sanctioned by the universe, a natural order of things that made the baby my grandbaby—and mine alone. My grandbaby wanted to make its presence known to me and knew that kissing its grandma was the best way to do it. I'll bet the baby knew that Grandma would never leave. Grandmas are always there for you, so they say! At that moment, I resolved that I would be there for my baby through thick and thin—another pact, by blood. I smiled at the thought.

I have often wondered what made some of my friends change from sane, loving, rational, and intelligent women to babbling, cooing puppets on a string, with every thought, word, and deed revolving around the grandbaby. Now I know. Oh my God! I'm now a doting grandma, one of "them," and the baby is yet to be born, it's just four months in utero!

All of this from a kiss in a dream! I'm convinced that my induction into "grandma-hood" places me in the noblest of sisterhoods. Looking forward to card-carrying membership in this special group makes me very happy.

Another Chance

Angie is not my baby anymore. She's all grown-up. She was a good child who had to grow up with a mother that loved her very much, but one who knew very little about nurturing and even less about mothering. Looking back, I think I was a very lucky woman. Though my husband and I divorced at a critical time in the lives of our two children, everything worked out just fine. Angela is a good person, she has a great career, and her husband comes from a good family. They respect each other as partners in their marriage.

It's a bit funny. Our children never fail to surprise us, even when they become adults. Angela and Jeffrey, as newlyweds, were so very proud of their status as DINKs (Dual Income, No Kids). What a very healthy place to be, I had thought when I first heard the acronym. They had no bills to speak of. They simply enjoyed their newfound relationship as husband and wife, and they enjoyed their freedom as a couple. Then, in a matter of a few months, it seemed that Angela became concerned that her reproductive clock was ticking away. Angela had told me of her desire to get pregnant during her visit home at Christmas. She had hoped to give Jeffrey a Christmas present in the form of a positive pregnancy test. It didn't work out as she had hoped, but after Christmas she seemed to be on a mission.

It didn't take long. In January, Angie knew she was pregnant; knew it, apparently, at the time of conception. She immediately had a blood test to confirm her suspicions. Then came the confirmation: she was going to have a baby! What a neat idea, I had thought—and left it at that. Even the confirmed announcement had not really sunk in.

Now, basking in the memory of the dream, I am hard-pressed to contain my joy.

I thought back to the day Angela had called to tell me the good news. I could hear her, as if she were actually speaking at that moment. When I had answered the call, she had asked, "Do you want your grandchild to call you 'Grand-darling' too?" That was a family tradition. I had called my mother's mother "Grand-darling" and my father's mother "Grand-dear," and Angie had called my mother, "Grand-darling." At the time, I was very happy for Angela, but had no special feelings of my own.

Now, that's all changed. Since the dream, it's as if there is this soft, rhythmic beat that beats in concert with my own heartbeat. This is so weird; so very, very weird.

In all of the happiness and pride that is associated with the first grandbaby, I did not want to overlook Angela. More than anything, I wanted her to bask in motherhood. I wanted her to get that early pregnancy glow; get that full face so common among pregnant women. And she did. She was so happy, and so was I.

But now, things have changed. I hadn't put things in perspective, before the dream. Now, when I touch her stomach, and when I see Angela touch her stomach, I remember the baby's kiss.

One day, when reflecting on this whole pregnancy experience, I had a nagging thought. After I had the dream, I talked to Angela the next day, but did not tell her about it. It was such a life-changing experience, and one that I had to share with Angela, yet I didn't even mention it. Why hadn't I shared such a wonderful moment? What was my motivation for not sharing?

Although I told Angela about the dream shortly thereafter, it was not until later that I realized why I had hesitated. Angela had always said that I loved her brother, James, more than I loved her. Somehow, inwardly, I had wondered if Angela would feel that I loved the baby more. It was in the middle of that thought that I had seen Angela's face in the face of the baby that kissed me. God's giving me another chance, I had thought. I get another chance to be a good mother to Angela through the life of her new baby. Through the kiss, Angela thanked me and the baby thanked me. It all became so very clear. In the face of the baby, I saw Angela, I saw myself, I saw my mother, and I saw my mother's mother. For the first time in a very long time, I loved myself, I forgave myself, and I paid homage to the mothers in my family, all of whom were a part of that special kiss.

We're Connected

Angela is only four months pregnant. I suppose you would think that's a long time, given the fact that this will be my first grandchild. Really, it's almost half of the time of this pregnancy, and I've just begun to give the "event" some serious thought.

I wonder what other first-time grandmothers feel. Everyone says that being a grandmother is such a special feeling, but what does a "grandmother with a grandbaby—in utero" actually feel?

Even when you consider the fact that I have just become emotionally involved in Angela's pregnancy, the truth is that I've always been emotionally involved in her pregnant condition. I've easily related to the morning sickness and the wonderful sensation of the baby's movements.

Now that the kiss has established an emotional connection to Angie's pregnancy, I find myself thinking about her a lot. She's really quite special. I know that women have been giving birth since the beginning of time, but this is different. I'm sure every expectant grandmother feels the same. In reality, my "little girl" is pregnant and the new baby will be her child. That's also very special. I'm often overwhelmed when I think about it. I'll bet that's why grandmothers everywhere feel so special about their grandchildren. Some people may argue that there are grandmothers who could not care less about the pregnancy of their daughter or about their unborn grandchild. I can't argue the point. Who could begin to understand why? I only know that there are times when I feel a sort of spiritual umbilical cord connection. You know what I mean. It's as if there is this invisible cord that runs from the baby to Angela to me. I can't describe the feeling. I just cannot describe it.

xoxoxoxo

Needing People

Last night, Angela showed her vulnerable self. I couldn't help her mood, nor did I understand it at the time, but it was real to her. It turns out that she had decided to spend the day shopping for maternity clothes and registering for gifts at a local store. Everywhere she went, other pregnant women in the maternity shops and the department stores had other people with them. Angela was alone because Jeffrey was on assignment and I was hundreds of miles away. Angela soon realized that this definitely was not an activity for a Saturday afternoon all by herself. She desperately needed her husband or her mom or her best friend to share in this moment. None of us were there, and that made her very sad. I think that was one of the low moments, so far, in an otherwise delightful pregnancy.

I think I'll suggest that she make a list of things about her pregnancy that make her feel helpless. Perhaps she can use the list to help other new mothers face this experience with an edge up on their emotions.

I wonder if unborn babies feel sad when their mothers feel sad. I'm sure there is some research somewhere that at least gives us an idea. In thinking about this situation, I get the distinct feeling that if Angela concentrates and asks the baby its opinion on buying clothes to fit her growing belly; if she silently converses with her baby about the outfits as she tries them on, she'll have a lot more fun shopping by herself. Somehow, she'll get a strong intuition about each outfit, I'm sure of it. Oh well, what do I know? I wish she were closer to me.

Hello, Grand-darling

Early in her pregnancy, Angie called to say that my grandchild did not like Chinese food. Um, looks like the baby's strong opinions came out, even as a fetus. Somehow, the baby sent Angie a message on anything in which its opinion was sought. I think, just to be sure, I'm going to make decision making one of my objectives in grand-parenting.

After not being totally involved in the pregnancy for almost four months, I suppose I could catch up by looking back at the time I've wasted during the pregnancy. How was I to know it would begin to mean so much? I'm sure that the baby's spirit has been with me from the start. What is unusual for me is the fact that I was not connected in ways that I would have envisioned I'd be—until now.

I suppose what's more important is that I am connected now, and I can look back at the past few months with a new perspective.

For example, the first time I saw a pregnant Angela, we were in Georgia at my mother's house. It was early spring and she was about three months along. As I remember seeing her face, I also remember seeing a definite glow about her. Her face was full, and her five-foot-eight, size 4 frame was now 120 pounds. But there was something else; something that I missed at the time. Now, in retrospect, there was something different. I know now that the baby was trying desperately to tell me, "I'm here, Grand-darling! I'm really here. Hello!"

Jessica Lauren

It's a girl. I'm going to have a granddaughter! In this modern age, more than enough information is available to expectant parents, including the sex of their unborn child. Angela and Jeff couldn't resist knowing. She sounded so happy when she told me. I was happy as well, and happy for her.

Knowing the baby would be a girl, we began the arduous task of selecting a name. I offered the name Jada, because my grandmother's name was Ada. With a J for Jeffrey, plus Ada—Jada. That didn't go over well with Jeff, Angie, or her brother, James. In fact, I was told that I didn't have a vote in deciding the name of the baby. Realistically, I couldn't blame them. I felt that way when I named Angela. So, after weeks of discussion, we (they did eventually ask my opinion) decided on Jessica Lauren.

Without knowing when it started, I began to daydream about my time with Jessica. More and more of the daydreams were about our being together when she is four or five years old. Often, we would be dancing and twirling with long flowing scarves, or spending time at the seashore searching for unusual seashells. I'm so excited! I look forward to just walking with her and holding her hand. I'll teach her to enjoy the beauty of silence.

"The Gods Love Nubia"

I saw her again. In a fleeting moment in my mind's eye, there she was. I was trying to take a nap and there she was. She looked like Jeffrey as a newborn, and then, in a flash, she was about seven years old. She was dressed in emerald green, my Nubian princess. She was in the back seat of a car, behind the driver. I don't know who the driver was. At seven, her looks were something of a cross between Angie and Lindsay, Angie's stepsister.

When Angie was growing up, after my divorce from her father, we used to eat breakfast, leave the dishes, go to the den, and listen to music. Often it was loud, but heck, it was the weekend and we were "bonding." We'd sing along to music from *The Wiz*, and a videotape of a Patti LaBelle special where she and Amy Grant sang "You Are My Friend." Man, that brings back so many wonderful, warm and fuzzy memories. We'd sing and cry and cry and sing well into the early afternoon. I think that much of Angie's inner strength as a young woman came from her passion for "Be a Lion" and "Home," two songs we always sang from *The Wiz*.

Heather Headley was on the *Today* show the other morning. She was singing one of the songs from the Broadway version of *Aida*; I think it was "Elaborate Lives." When I heard it, I began to reminisce about our weekend singing sessions. I can't wait to have those sessions with Jessica. We're going to have so much fun and she'll learn so much. After all, as Elton John and Tim Rice wrote, "The Gods Love Nubia."

xoxoxoxo

Boy or Girl

Today, Angie told me that a nurse practitioner questioned her about the ultrasound, suggesting that, in her opinion, the baby's heartbeat was slow, and boys have slower heartbeats. It's amazing how such news puts a different perspective on all of this. For some time now, I've been reacting to thoughts and plans centered on a girl. Things change so much when, all of a sudden, thoughts and plans center on a boy. How will I bond with this male grandchild?

Girl babies are so delicate. I see them through soft, fuzzy lenses. As future grandmothers, somewhere in our lineage, in our history, we share a precious bond with our granddaughters. That's a guess on my part, since I'm new at this grandmother thing.

Boy babies are so precious. I see them through very clear lenses. Precise, in contrast to how we sense and feel our girl babies.

In reality, for those of us who have raised both girl and boy babies with the same rules, as I have done, it's hard to define or justify these unusual feelings I have about a future granddaughter, as opposed to a future grandson. In any case, we'll play, whirling around with our eyes closed, searching for seashells on the seashore, listening to and singing along with music—boy or girl.

The Brown Linen Dress with Jacket

Can you believe it? Angie called to say that she needed to borrow some of my clothes, especially my long linen dresses, to use as maternity clothes. I should have been highly insulted, but I understood her thinking. Did I mention that Angie hates to spend her money? She has no problem spending my money, but major depression sets in when the dollars come out of her wallet!

So, when she asked, I understood. She would save money. Never mind the fact that her usual size 4 would now look fine in my size 12s and 14s. I sent them to her like a dutiful and caring mother. I was glad to do it.

Later, after she had received the package of dresses, I had yet another connection to my unborn grandchild. I was literally playing a part in this pregnancy. I was clothing the pregnant belly of my daughter. Dresses that I had loved and worn were now serving a purpose in the development of my grandbaby. When Angie wore my dress and rubbed her belly, she was, in a way, creating a sense of belonging for the three of us. She called me the day she wore my favorite—the brown linen dress with matching jacket. When I get it back, it'll be my favorite with a very special meaning.

xoxoxoxo

Getting There

My mom is ninety years old. Angie's baby will be her first great-grandchild. We want to be with Angie when the baby is born. We live on the East Coast, and Jeff and Angie recently moved to California. After much discussion, Mom wants to take the train. On Amtrak's new superliner, she'll get a chance to see the country and go to California for the first time.

I even took a superliner to Chicago and got a glimpse of how we'd travel. The trip was one of the most relaxing trips I had ever had. I met lots of interesting people and had time to read, write, and enjoy the beautiful scenery.

Getting tickets for the train trip was most difficult. We literally had to pick an available date and hope the baby did not come before we got there. Angie's due date is October 23. We are scheduled to arrive on October 24. I sure hope the baby holds off until we get there.

I'm so excited. All my friends tell me how wonderful the experience will be. Bobbie, a colleague, says she gets goose bumps just thinking about her grandchild. Other friends have told me that it's an experience unlike any other. I keep hoping that Angie doesn't have the baby before we get there. I'd truly hate not being with her for this wonderful event. We're in the countdown. Hold on, my darling baby. Grand-darling really wants you to wait for *her* arrival before *your* arrival.

Matters of the Heart

On October 13, 2000, I had emergency triple bypass surgery. In my nightmares I remember minor chest pains, tests, more tests, and then the big one, a cardiac catheterization. From there, it was all downhill. I was not to go home; I was to be placed in an ambulance, driven to another hospital, and scheduled for the emergency surgery the next day.

In this nightmare, I could not imagine that I had coronary artery disease. Not me. I faithfully went to the fitness center, I tried to eat right, and I played golf every weekend. I'm only fifty-six years old, for Christ's sake! I'm a woman in perpetual motion, the epitome of health! This must be a dream. It wasn't.

I remember thinking that this couldn't be happening. I also remember a funny feeling in my chest. And lately, I had been so very tired, especially when I exercised. Something really was wrong.

I also realized that something else was definitely wrong. My baby would have her baby without me. I cried when I heard the news. I cried during the ambulance ride to the other hospital. I cried myself to sleep that night before the surgery. What would she do without me? What would I do without her? This was a once-in-a-lifetime event. I was supposed to be with her. I prayed for another dream of my grandbaby, but my prayers were not answered. This was truly a matter of the heart. My heart was broken.

xoxoxoxo

The Wait

Grandma, Grand-darling to be, was almost not to be. I had good news and good news: they found it and they fixed it. The gravity of the situation was not lost on any of us. My son drove up from Florida, picking up my mother in Georgia on the way. My daughter and her husband recognized that this little setback would improve my chances of being around for their baby. We settled back and waited; waited for me to heal and for the baby to make his or her entrance.

My son, James, stayed with me for a week. He was a comfort and a help to my husband, Richard, during this ordeal. They're buddies, and they were a wonderful comfort to me during my hospital stay. Driving home on the day of my discharge from the hospital, Richard, true to his nature, took us on a sightseeing trip around Norfolk. We had to ride by Ocean View Golf Course, where we had been chaperones for Tiger Woods' exhibition just a few weeks before. I love playing golf. I was told that I can't play until spring. My husband, my son, my mother, all of us together in a car full of beautiful flowers; my surgery had been successful and I was already envisioning golf in the spring. I thought, I'm a lucky woman! It was a beautiful day and a beautiful ride home.

Angie and Jeff called every day, and every day was one more day to get used to the fact that I would not be with her when the baby was born. Angie promised to call me whenever it was time to leave for the hospital, day or night.

The initial call came at seven thirty in the morning my time, and four thirty her time. She had had active cramps all night and they were getting ready to head to the hospital. Not to worry, they had taken Lamaze classes and Jeff was a good coach. Everything would be all right. They would call me.

The first call came about three thirty that afternoon. It had been a long day of waiting to become a grandma. Was the baby here? Not yet. Angie had the epidural, but no serious move on the baby's part. They'd call again. Oh my, I thought, this long day was getting longer. We played telephone tag; Jeff's mom, Angie's paternal grandmother, and I. "Nothing yet, I'll call," became our mantra.

The Call

The real call came at seven thirty that night. They had discovered that the baby was in a breech position. The doctor has decided to do a Cesarean section delivery. They'd be out in about an hour. Jeff would call me and I could call everybody else.

Another turn of events! Angie had exercised and done everything to be in shape for her delivery. Now, she had to have a surgical delivery. What would she do without me? How would she care for the baby after her surgery, which would limit her strength and mobility? I began to pray.

An hour passed with no phone call. Jeff's mom called me. Angie's father called me. No word. Two hours passed, and still no word from Jeff. Lord, what had gone wrong? I tried to stay in a positive frame of mind, but couldn't stop thinking that Jeff really should have called by then. Angie's father called again. "What is the name of the hospital?" he asked. "Surely someone there knows what is going on."

Around ten p.m., Angie's father called back; he had found them. He called with the news that a baby girl had been born, and they were just getting to a private room. I sighed a deep sigh of relief and said a silent prayer of gratitude. My baby and her baby were all right, and I was a grandma.

xoxoxoxo

So Excited, Can't Hide It

This one event was so exciting for all of us. When I called James to tell him the news, Charmell, his wife, began to bounce on the bed for joy, but he was rather reserved. As it turned out, he had been holding out for a nephew, while she had been betting on a niece. Even when they had shopped for clothes, he had actually bought outfits for a little boy. I smiled at the image of Charmell bouncing on the bed. As we talked, it was hard to imagine that my son was in his own home with his wife, and that my daughter and her husband had just had a child of their own.

I got a very nice card from Jeffrey's mom—congratulations to a new grandmother. I hadn't thought of sending her one. She's so thoughtful. I suppose after five children and several grandchildren, she knew the ropes. I knew that would come in handy in the days and months to come. It had been thirty-three years since I had a baby.

Angie and I talked every day. She relayed the events of each day during our telephone conversations. She described little things, like Jeffrey holding the baby in his arms and Jessica staring up at him in awe. I thought that Jessica must have been saying to herself, "This is really something. One day it's all dark, and the next day I see my daddy. I think I'm in love." At least that's the picture I got. Angie said that Jessica had initiated a bonding ritual already—and already, Daddy was hooked.

Life is wonderful. I have a daughter that I love; her husband loves her, and he loves their baby. Many women are not that lucky, either as mothers or as grandmothers. Or babies, for that matter, whether they be boy or girl.

xoxoxoxo

Homecoming

It was Thursday, and Jessica, Angela, and Jeffrey were going home. Angie had told me that Jessica was a favorite in the nursery and everyone would miss her. The nurses had put a ribbon in her hair for the trip home. In my heart, I knew that they probably had said those words and done the ribbon thing many times over. Still, I hoped that all of the sweet compliments and nice gestures were actually because Jessica was special, very special.

Not long after they had arrived home and settled in, Jessica began to cry. We thought it was because the house was drafty, so Jeff and Angie swaddled her tightly and looked forward to their first night at home with their new baby.

That first night was rough. Jessica cried most of the night and they got little sleep. This was not good for Angie, especially since she had come home and tried to do too much. You know, the things that a new mother just has to do, like put the letters J-E-S-S-I-C-A on the curtain rod in the nursery as a finishing touch to her decorating. She'd had a C-section, remember. She actually pushed herself too far. My heart ached to be with her.

For several days, I followed the lives of my grandbaby and her mom and dad through phone conversations. We experienced the first poop, sore nipples, irritated stitches in Angie's abdomen, uncomfortable feeding positions, and Jessica's loss of weight. All the while, Jessica cried or was a less than calm and contented baby.

Angie's voice took on a tired and sad tone. She was overwhelmed. I knew better than to question God and His wisdom, but my baby really needed me. She still needed me and I could not be there to help. Jeffrey was wonderful. He had taken paternity leave, and he truly pampered her, cooked for her, and more. The problem was, my little "goddess of perfection" knew that things were not so perfect. None of this was what she had envisioned. To make matters worse, she was bordering on depression because of the C-section. She had worked so hard to make sure she was in shape for a normal delivery, to make sure everything was right. Now, every day she faced a scar on her abdomen that was not healing properly. A scar! I'm sure she was heading for the "why me?" syndrome. All of this had become something that truly made her sad.

I didn't know what to say to her. I knew that nothing I said would make it better. All I could do was trust the things that she had been taught. She was a lion. She had courage. She had fortitude. She had faith in God. I had to trust her spirit. For me, that was easy to do.

xoxoxoxo

Breaking the Code

It was a light-bulb moment. In the wee hours of the morning, when Jeff and Angie were dealing with an uncomfortable and unhappy Jessica, Angie had tried the breast pump. Less than one ounce had come from one breast and virtually none from the other. As a last resort, they had tried using some of the infant formula, part of the complimentary gifts they had received when Angie was discharged from the hospital, as a supplement.

Jessica drank three ounces, went to sleep, and woke up, as Angie described it, as if she had eaten Thanksgiving dinner. Clearly, Jessica had been crying and irritable because she had not been getting enough milk from her mother's breasts. Our little baby was hungry—and had been hungry for days. Thank God for small miracles. I had begun to worry that something was really wrong.

Now, she's like a new baby. Jessica sits quietly in her swing, coos, and smiles. She is a calm and contented baby.

It's a new day for Angie, too. Despite the earlier trials, which were very real to her, she sounds like herself now. She even ventured out with Jessica the other day for a trip in the car. They were in search of a baby-wipe warmer. Yes, it's true, they now make baby-wipe warmers, and there is such a demand for these that the store had sold out! In my day, we used warm washcloths! Angie promptly informed me that a warm baby-wipe is very convenient for those early morning changes. Having one of those warmers on hand would be great. I've got so much to learn. This new role is going to be a whole lot of fun.

xoxoxoxo

Love Conquers Fear

I love my Jessica. I am fearful of flying. But because of my love for Jessica, I have made plans to fly across the country to see her. Jeffrey told me to take out a picture of Jessica whenever I feel frightened during the flight.

I want to see Jessica so much. Jeffrey will be away for a week or so on a work-related assignment, so Mom and I are flying out to stay with Angie. From the time that we decided to go, I have been preparing myself for the trip. I don't know when I actually began to hate flying, but my fear is real to me. This trip will be a true test of my faith.

Our flight was scheduled for six a.m. My daughter-in-law, Charmell, flies a lot as part of her job. She suggested that

I stay up all night so I would sleep during the flight. I did my best with about two hours of sleep.

Thank God we had an uneventful flight. We had to change planes twice, with a five-hour stint between Dulles and Los Angeles. I prayed a lot, called on the spirits of many of my dead relatives, and invoked a special request for safety to all of my fairies and angels. I also kept Jessica's picture in view. We had a wonderful flight.

When we arrived at Santa Maria and deplaned, Angie and Jessica were nowhere to be found. I wondered where they could be. As we entered the terminal, I got an answer to my question. There stood Angie, with a camera to capture my expression as my eyes roamed in search of Jessica. Against a wall in the terminal was the beautiful car seat that held my beautiful granddaughter. Attached to the car seat was a big pink sign that read "Happy Birthday!" My birthday was the day before our arrival, but that didn't matter. Grand-darling was soon to get her kiss, in person. What a wonderful birthday present!

xoxoxoxo

Getting to Know You

Getting to know my Jessica was heaven for me. During my visit, I slept in her room, learned how to change a disposable diaper, used warm baby-wipes, helped with her baths, selected outfits from the closet full of clothes her mother had arranged, and fed her. I couldn't get enough of my Jessica.

Pretty soon, I had the routine down pat. I talked to her, I sang to her, I whispered to her and smiled at her, I burped her and I put her to sleep. I tried to comfort her when she cried, and reluctantly turned her over to her mom when absolutely necessary. I became possessive and eager to get her back when her great-grandmother held her. All I wanted was my Jessica. Many days, I knew that I had overdone it a bit when my sternum, still weak from the bypass operation, ached painfully. I tried to slow down a bit, but Angie did need some rest and I wanted to help.

We took "hundreds" of pictures and had "hundreds" of reprints made. Every day, we headed out to get more film and have more reprints developed for ourselves and for family. We had great fun. We shopped for Christmas decorations and for Jeff's birthday. We decorated the house and watched Baby Einstein videotapes with Jessica. Jeff's commander had Santa flown in for a Christmas party for the children and families of his squadron. I wrapped Jessica's first Christmas present (I took a picture of it), and saw her in Santa's arms for the first time (another picture, of course!).

Speaking of pictures, our visit was almost over and we had yet to have a four-generation portrait taken. At the last minute, we got a walk-in appointment at Wal-Mart. We dressed Jessica in a beautiful outfit and headed off to have the portrait made.

I don't think I've mentioned the fact that Jessica had what I called "growing days." On those days, she slept soundly for hours. This happened to be one of those days, and when we arrived for the portrait, Jessica was sound asleep!

The photographer had a very difficult time keeping her awake for the picture. She looked so precious that onlookers started to take part in our efforts to keep her awake and make her smile. One woman got so involved that she proceeded to give us directions as to how to sit and hold Jessica. The photographer was quite patient and we ended up with beautiful proofs. Four generations, from ninety years old to six weeks old! We are blessed indeed.

xoxoxoxo

Four Generations

Tonight I'm babysitting for Jeff and Angela. They, deservedly, are having a night out for a Christmas party. Actually, I'm babysitting the youngest member of the family and the oldest member of the family. Both Mom and Jessica are sleeping.

I have two more days here, and then I'm heading for home. My visit has been incredible! Mom, Angie, Jessica, and I have interacted in such a wonderful way. Three strong, outspoken black women and a fourth generation baby girl!

As we shared this wonderful occasion, family dynamics that go back for generations surfaced in our conversations and interactions. At one point, Angie wisely suggested that the qualifying statement "in my opinion" precede our comments. Our family members are known for putting in their two cents for every situation.

Four generations: happy, humble, very proud, and very outspoken. During this visit, we've all received our kisses, shared smiles and laughter, and made stronger the link by which our lives and lineage will be remembered. What a wonderful gift from God!

In the final days of our visit, we packed a picnic lunch and drove to Santa Barbara. The trip down the Central Coast was beautiful. I fell in love with the mountains and seashore; tourists, residents and quaint shops; young carolers and sailboats at a marina; birds and a sunset over the Pacific. I fell in love with Jessica. I fell in love with being a grandma.

xoxoxoxo

Time to Say Good-bye

I hope there will be many good-byes for Jessica and me. Good-byes for us will most likely mean the end of a few stolen days together. But, they will also hold the promise of new and wonderful days together for years to come.

The days passed swiftly as we prepared to return home. On our last night, we went out to dinner at Saletti's, a wonderful Italian restaurant in Lompoc. Many of the people in the restaurant were captivated by Jessica. She was captivated by them as well. For the most part, she sat quietly as we ate, constantly watching the waiters and waitresses as they went about their jobs.

When we got home, my time with Jessica was reflective. I found myself staring at her in an effort to imprint her expressions in my memory. As I held her, I felt a tug of emotions when I noticed how her small hand held on to my thumb. I think I even asked Angie to take a picture of her holding on to me.

The next morning found me in solemn spirits. In addition to my anxiety about the flight, the thought of leaving Jessica was overwhelming. Angie brought her to me for some special time together before we left for the airport. I held her and we talked about my visit. I really didn't want to leave her.

We arrived quite early for check-in, so we all had breakfast and made light conversation. I had asked Jeff about the plane that would fly us to L.A. He said it was relatively new, and he encouraged me to look into the cockpit when I got on the plane. He was sure I'd be impressed. When our flight was announced, Angie took a picture of me giving Jessica a good-bye kiss, our first. Mom and I gave our final hugs and left to board the plane.

I had a wonderful time with my daughter and her family. I had a special time with Jessica. I wondered if she would be crawling or walking when I saw her next. What would she look like?

As the airplane accelerated for takeoff, I took one last look at the airport and the window where I imagined they'd be:

my family, my Jessica. The plane lifted into the air and my eyes filled with tears. I missed her already.

Jessica came to me in a dream, at first. Now, she is my precious granddaughter. Our love started with a kiss. Now, she has my heart. She is my heart.

xoxoxoxo

Epilogue

And another…

Olivia was born in August 2002 at RAF Lakenheath, Suffolk, United Kingdom. Mom, Richard, and I took the long flight over the Atlantic for the glorious event. Another grandbaby! Another precious little person who, for the rest of her life, would call me Grand-darling.

In so many ways, I've grown into my role as grandma, and in so many ways I feel as though it's my first day on the job. It's been such a wonderful time, these past seven and a half years. I've done most of the things I said I'd do, with Jessica and Olivia.

We've sung songs, old and new, and mostly Disney. We've played games, let the sunshine in, taken deep breaths of fresh air, caressed and smelled flowers, enjoyed the silence of meditation and guided imagery, sought seashells on the beach, gone to a baseball game, and played golf. I've taught them to touch their "courage button" and know that they can do anything they want to do, with Mom and Dad's permission. Jeff and Angie are wonderful parents. He has been to Iraq five times, and Angie homeschooled this year.

Mom died in February 2004. She was ninety-three years old. We miss her so much, but all of us understand, so well, the joy and true meaning "grandma," "mama," and "child." We all get second chances. Some second chances begin with a kiss.

xoxoxoxo

Made in the USA